# Mr. Jay's Bac

T0040393

David Rodriguez
Illustrated by Gaston Vanzet

Mr. Jay had a bad day.
In the morning, the faucet broke.

"Oh, no!" said Mr. Jay.
"I need to call for help."

The plumber came.
She fixed the faucet.

In the afternoon, Mr. Jay's car wouldn't start.

"Oh, no!" said Mr. Jay.
"I need to call for help."

The mechanic came.
He fixed the car.

JAY

In the evening, Mr. Jay dropped his dinner.

"Oh, no!" said Mr. Jay.
"What should I do?"